Angels In The Clouds
By: Jennifer April Danny

www.angelsintheclouds.com

Copyright ©2009 Jennifer April Danny

Notice Of Rights
All rights reserved. No part of this book may be reproduced or transmitted in any form, by any means, electronic, mechanical, photocopying or otherwise, without the prior written permission of the author.

Publisher: Jennifer Danny

ISBN: 978-0692681381

www.**angelsintheclouds**.com | Email: jennifer@angelsintheclouds.com

Design & Layout - MDPD Design (661) 373-0300

Angels In The Clouds

One afternoon I was sitting in my car and noticed a beautiful cloud formation behind the nearby buildings. I watched as the wind blew it into it's intended figure...that of an angel. I took a picture and shared it with my family and friends.

The photograph was featured in a magazine along with an article I had written about my recent "angel discoveries". I relished in my new journey of seeing these magnificent 'angel clouds' and before I knew it I had enough for a book. Here they are for your viewing pleasure, I bet you'll never look at a cloud in the same way again!

Jennifer April Danny

"Baby Cherub"

(look on the right side of the cloud formation)

Swiftly moving, hands outstretched

as her Angel body takes form.

"Angel With Wings" after a cloud-filled rainy day. This angel appeared. Look for his outline and you can see he's facing the opposite way of the sign that reads: "One Way" with the arrow. I think it's a reminder to go the 'way of angels'.

Angel above shower us with your love.

Look at each formation and see, what kind of angel you'd like it
to be! The contrast of blue against the light allows
each angel cloud to come into sight.

Angel Poem

" I chanced upon a cloud above, most certain the feeling was that of pure love"

"So I continued my journey in the hopes I would see,
more of God's beings looking for me"

" Up in the sky, some hidden from view, ready to delight a skeptic, or two"

"There they stay, among the blue and white, guiding the day into the night"

" So be gracious to each other, even if it's someone you don't recognize,
as a wise man once said:

"All of God's Angels Come to Us In Disguise"

Love Jennifer

Take flight dear angels so far away you roam,
soaring higher and higher to carry me home!

Sky of blue, angel of white, lead the way with your guiding light.

Let your imagination be your guide. An "angel in the cloud" extends its wing and beckons you to come along for the ride.

Angel bird clouds on a perch.

Angel clouds dancing in twilight!

Follow your heart and look toward the sky,
there is no limit as to what greets your eye!

They comfort us in time of need,
Angels abound, just let your mind lead.

Ethereal Beings!

Polar Bear Angel Clouds!

A mother angel cloud and her baby.

Under the Angel's wings, I am protected and loved.

Angels Ascending!

Feather white wings, that cover and shield,
never doubt the wonder their protection can yield.

White against gray outlining the sky,
angel clouds forming as they gracefully float by.

Hummingbird Angel Clouds.

How Many Angels Can You Find?

Look to the top left. Do you see a face?
Arm is outstretched as the angels take place.

White wisps of wonder dancing up high,
the sun captures their light in the afternoon sky.

Angels going home!

www.ingramcontent.com/pod-product-compliance
Lightning Source LLC
Chambersburg PA
CBHW041745040426
42444CB00001B/34